Contents

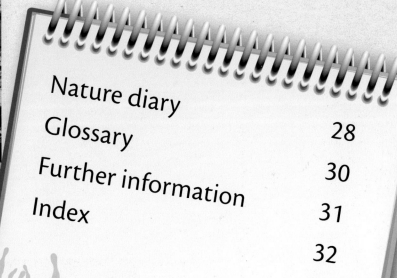

At the seaside

The seaside is the place where the land meets the ocean. Many different kinds of scenery can be found here, including cliffs, rocky shores, sand or pebble beaches, **dunes** and mudflats. Each of these places provides a **habitat** for different plants and animals.

Rockpools on the beach are like mini-aquariums, with many plants and animals.

This is a sandy beach.

4

Seaside

Jen Green

Photographs by Emma Solley

9030 00002 0112 8

First published in 2010 by Wayland

Copyright © Wayland 2010

This paperback edition published in 2011
by Wayland

Wayland
338 Euston Road
London NW1 3BH

Wayland Australia
Level 17/207 Kent Street
Sydney, NSW 2000

Senior editor: Camilla Lloyd
Designer: Phipps Design
Photographer: Emma Solley
Illustrator: Peter Bull

British Library Cataloguing in Publication Data:
Green, Jen.
  Seaside. – (Nature trail)
  1. Seashore ecology–Juvenile literature.
  2. Seashore animals–Juvenile literature.
  3. Seashore plants–Juvenile literature.
  I. Title II. Series
  577.6'99-dc22

ISBN: 978 0 7502 6744 1

Printed in China

Wayland is a division of Hachette Children's Books, an Hachette UK company.
www.hachette.co.uk

Animals such as this crab are shy and good at hiding, so you have to look carefully. Sudden movements will scare animals away.

This symbol warns when extra care is needed. Always take care of nature. Never pick flowers. If you handle small creatures, treat them gently.

On the trail

On the nature trail at the seaside you will need a hat, sunglasses, sun cream and sandals or wellies.

hat

sunglasses

sun cream

strong shoes or boots

waterproof clothing

Make notes and drawings using a notebook, pen and coloured pencils. A magnifying glass, binoculars, camera, fishing net and a container can be useful.

magnifying glass

notebook and pen

coloured pencils

ice cream container

fishing net

binoculars

Between the tides

Twice a day, the sea moves up the shore and then falls back again. These changes are called **tides**. Seaside plants and animals have to cope with ever-changing conditions, as they are covered with salty seawater and then left high and dry.

The beach is the area between the high and low tide mark. Different plants and animals live at different levels on the beach.

At high tide waves lap at the top of the beach. The lowest part of the beach is covered with water except at very low tide.

Always find out what the tide is doing. The tide can rise quickly over a flat beach. The times of the tides are different every day.

A line of seaweed, shells and other debris is left at the high tide mark – the highest level reached by the waves.

What do you see?

Walk from the top of the beach down towards the water. The upper, middle and lower shore have different plants and animals. Use your notebook to record the plants and animals you see in each zone.

Was it high or low tide when you visited the seaside?

On the cliffs

Cliffs form where a line of hills meets the sea. Clifftops are often grassy, and dotted with flowers in spring and summer. Rabbits live in clifftop burrows. Seabirds perch on ledges half-way down!

What do you see?

Binoculars will help you study cliff birds. A bird book can help you to identify them. What were the birds doing?

Seabirds such as these black-headed gulls nest on cliffs where their eggs and young are safe from most enemies.

Different types of birds nest on the cliffs.

Puffins nest in burrows near the top of cliffs.

Guillemots lay their eggs on narrow ledges.

Kittiwakes build seaweed nests on steep cliffs.

Gannets raise one chick in a seaweed nest.

Clifftop plants have to cope with strong winds and salty air. This plant is called thrift.

⚠ Cliff edges can crumble away. Never stand close to the edge, or on the beach directly below.

Gorse grows on the cliff edge.

Insects visit clifftop plants for food.

9

Pebble beach

Pebbles on the beach are made of rocks worn smooth by the waves. The stones mostly come from local cliffs, or have been swept along the coast by the tide.

Pebble beaches are home to tough plants that can stand salty conditions, and birds such as ringed plovers.

Plants that grow among the pebbles make do with very little soil. This is sea bindweed.

As the waves lap against the pebbles on the beach they become more smooth.

Can you find any pebbles that are not made of stone?

⚠ Beware of broken glass or rusty cans that could cut you.

As waves grind small chunks of rock, they become smooth, rounded pebbles.

What do you see?

Make a collection of pebbles. Most pebbles are probably made of one type of rock. Can you see the rocks on nearby cliffs?

The remains of cuttlefish are called cuttlebone. They can be found amongst the pebbles on some beaches.

11

Birds on the shore

Birds that live at the seaside find their food in different places. Terns and gannets dive underwater to catch fish. Oystercatchers wade at the water's edge. Turnstones hunt at the high-tide mark.

Birds have beaks, legs and feet of different shapes, which helps them move about and catch their food.

The herring gull's **webbed feet** push against the water. Birds with webbed feet are strong swimmers.

What do you see?

Prints in the sand can be used to identify birds. Compare the prints you find with the ones shown here. You may also see prints made by animals such as dogs, horses – and people!

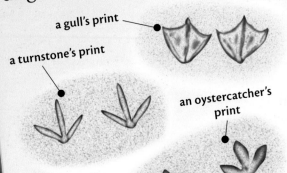

a gull's print

a turnstone's print

an oystercatcher's print

Do most of the birds you see on the seashore have webbed feet?

12

These birds can be found on the seashore. You might see the prints of these birds on the sand.

A herring gull's hooked beak grips slippery fish.

A turnstone overturns pebbles in search of food.

An oystercatcher probes for worms with its long bill.

This is a black-headed gull.

Young seagulls have different coloured feathers to the adults.

Plants of the sea

Seaweeds are the main group of plants found at the seashore. There are also tiny floating plants called **plankton**. These sea plants don't have stems, leaves and roots like the plants you see on land. But like all plants, they need sunlight to live and grow.

Seaweed can make rocks slippery so take care when walking on rocks and around rockpools.

What do you see?

Different types of seaweed live at different levels on the beach. For example, kelp and oarweed are only seen at low tide. How many types of seaweed can you spot on your way down to the sea?

This seaweed is brown kelp. Seaweeds such as kelp anchor themselves to rocks using a root-like part called a **holdfast**.

Yellow-brown bladderwrack live half-way down the beach. Air-filled pouches called bladders help the **fronds** to float.

frond

bladder

Seaweeds come in three main colours: red, green and brown. What colour are the ones you see?

Small fish can sometimes be seen swimming among the seaweed. Some fish and many other creatures feed on tiny floating plants called plankton.

In the sand

Sand is made from tiny bits of rock and shell that have been smashed to pieces by the waves. A sandy beach can look bare and lifeless, but worms, shellfish and many other creatures are hidden in the sand.

Shells can be found on sandy beaches. These are cockle shells.

These worms and shellfish hide in the sand.

A lugworm lives in a U-shaped burrow.

A sand mason's burrow has a frilly top.

A razor shell leaves two tiny holes at the surface.

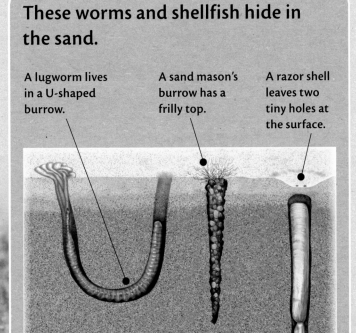

What do you see?

Locate burrowing animals from the signs they leave at the surface. You could dig down quickly to find the burrower. Put it in a bucket of seawater to study it. Then put it back gently and watch it dig down again.

Lugworms swallow sand and filter out small bits of food. The waste sand is squeezed out to leave a squiggly heap at the surface.

Crabs also burrow in the sand. Crabs are scavengers – they eat whatever they can find.

Among the dunes

The wind blows loose sand to the back of the beach. There it piles up to make heaps called sand dunes. Grass and other plants root among the dunes. Some seabirds and many kinds of minibeasts live here.

Marram grass has long roots to gather moisture. The roots also help to **anchor** the sand.

What do you see?

Make drawings of the plants you see in your notebook. First, look carefully at the shape of leaves, stems and flowers. Add colour using pencils or pens.

Dune plants such as this thistle have tough, leathery leaves that keep in moisture. This prevents the plant from drying out in the salty air.

Minibeasts such as bees and butterflies feed on flower nectar. Spiders and ladybirds **prey** on other minibeasts.

How many different minibeasts can you see in the dunes?

In the shallows

All sorts of amazing creatures live in the shallow waters just offshore. You will see them only at very low tide, or if they get washed up on the beach by accident. These animals spend all or most of their time underwater.

Oystercatchers hunt for shellfish on the rocks at low tide.

What do you see?

Barnacles close up out of water. Put a small rock or pebble with a barnacle on it into a bucket of seawater and watch what happens. Limpets look fixed in one place, but at high tide they move about. Put a blob of paint on a living limpet shell to identify it. Note its exact position and see if it moves as the sea rises or falls.

Each limpet has a home base – a little groove in the rock. At high tide it moves about to eat seaweed.

Mussels can be found stuck to the rocks at low tide.

In a shell

Many seaside animals live inside a shell that protects their soft bodies. They are known as shellfish, and there are two main groups. Sea-snails such as whelks, periwinkles and scallops are **molluscs**.

Crabs, shrimps and lobsters belong to a different group, called **crustaceans**. These many-legged creatures have a hard skin, like body armour.

These mollusc shells often wash up on the seashore.

periwinkle

scallop

limpet

razor clam

Lobsters are crustaceans with huge front claws and a hard body case.

Unlike other crabs the hermit crab has a soft body, so it hides inside an old mollusc shell.

What do you see?

Make a collection of shells. Make sure no one is still living inside! Wash the shells in fresh water and leave them outdoors for a day or so to dry. Group your finds according to shape.

What shape are most of the shells you have found?

A cockle has a double shell joined by a strong **hinge**. It burrows into soft sand.

23

In a rockpool

Rockpools form on rocky beaches when the tide goes out, leaving pools of salt water. Many different living things are found in rockpools, including seaweeds, jelly-like anemones, prawns, molluscs, starfish, crabs and small fish.

Rockpools contain dozens of different living things, both large and small.

Try this!

Study rockpool life by gently sweeping your net across the pool and along the bottom. Put the creatures in a container filled with seawater while you look at them. You could use a magnifying glass. Put them back when you have finished.

Take care on slippery rocks. Beware of rising tides.

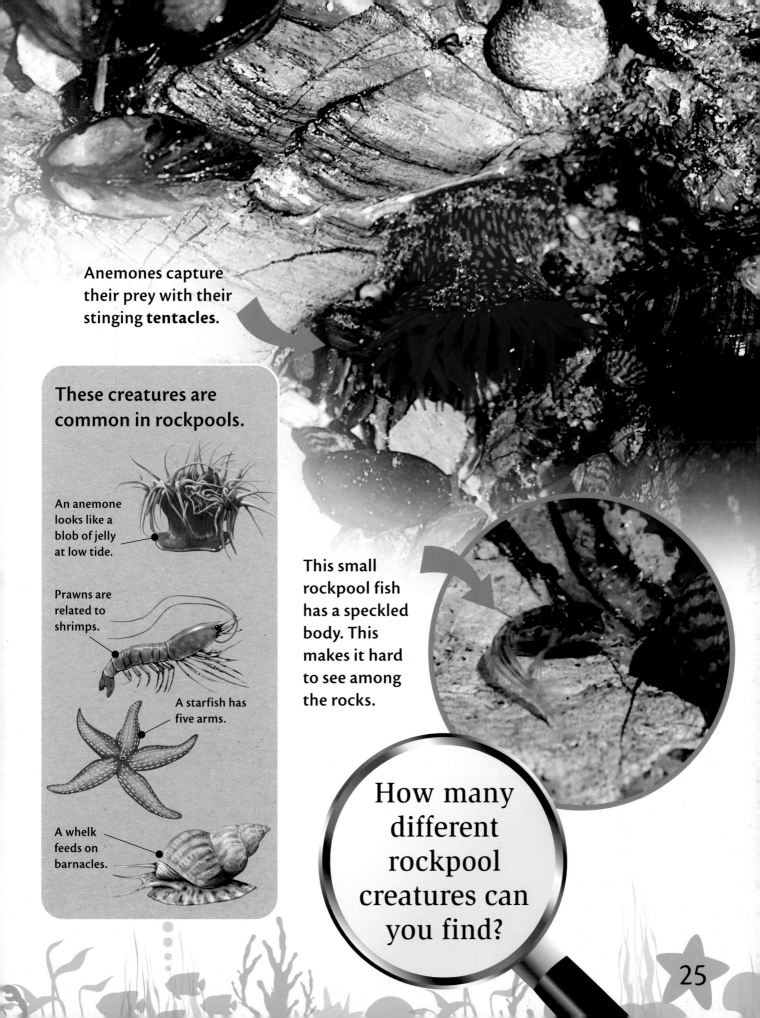

Anemones capture their prey with their stinging **tentacles**.

These creatures are common in rockpools.

An anemone looks like a blob of jelly at low tide.

Prawns are related to shrimps.

A starfish has five arms.

A whelk feeds on barnacles.

This small rockpool fish has a speckled body. This makes it hard to see among the rocks.

How many different rockpool creatures can you find?

Seaside food chains

Living things on the seashore depend on one another for food. Diagrams called food chains show who eats what. Plants form the base of seaside food chains. They provide food for animals called **herbivores**. These may be eaten by meat-eating hunters, known as **carnivores**.

This gull is eating a crab. Crabs feed on sandhoppers – shrimp-like creatures that eat rotting seaweed at the high tide mark.

This food chain shows the links between the gull, crab, sandhopper and seaweed. The gull is the carnivore at the top of the chain.

Look around you and see if you can spot animals eating plants or other creatures. Try to draw a food chain showing the animals. You need to know what each animal eats.

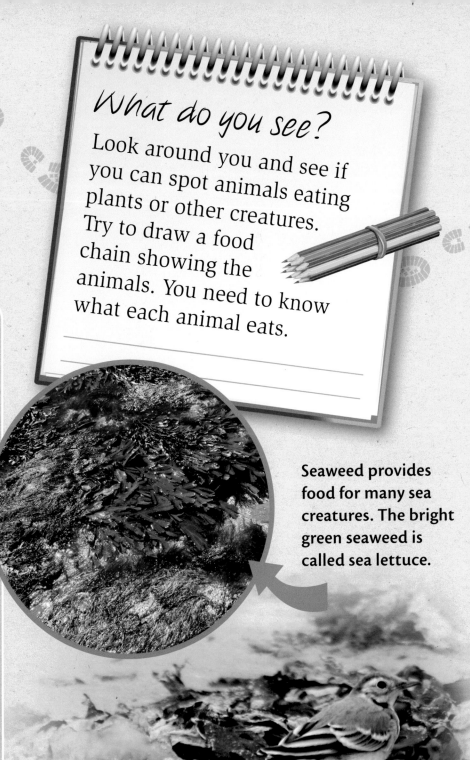

The gull eats the crab.

The crab eats the sandhopper.

The sandhopper eats the seaweed.

Seaweed provides food for many sea creatures. The bright green seaweed is called sea lettuce.

This long-tailed bird, a pied wagtail, is searching for food among the seaweed.

Nature diary

Build up a detailed picture of life on the seashore in your notebook. Add drawings or photos. All sorts of amazing things wash up on beaches. Each fresh tide brings new treasures. Start your own collection.

KEEP NOTES

Always take your notebook with you. Note the date, time, weather, state of the tide and exact location. Describe and sketch what you see.

Date: **11 August**

Time: 9am

Weather: Sunny

Tide: Low tide

Location: Beach rockpools

Observations: Saw sea lettuce in large rockpool and anemones in small rockpool.

Can you identify these rockpool creatures? If you see a plant or animal you don't recognise, make notes and a sketch or take a photo. Look it up later in a book about seashore life.

TOP TIPS

● Use the cover of rocks or sand dunes to approach birds and animals without being noticed.

● Try not to let your shadow fall on rockpools, as it will give you away and creatures will hide from you.

BEACHCOMBING

Beach finds include smooth driftwood, shells, pebbles, crab claws, feathers and seaweed. You can collect your finds in a bucket. Can you identify your finds?

Glossary

anchor To hold something firmly in place.

carnivore An animal that eats meat.

crustacean One of a group of animals with many legs and a hard body case, such as lobsters, crabs and shrimps.

dune A mound of wind-blown sand, found at the back of a beach.

frond Part of a seaweed that is like a stem and leaves.

habitat The natural home of plants or animals, such as a wood or the seashore.

herbivore An animal that eats plants.

hinge The joint where two parts of something are held together. One part can swing or open away from the other.

holdfast A root-like part used by seaweed to anchor onto rocks.

mollusc A shelled animal such as a clam, whelk or winkle.

plankton Tiny floating plants and animals that are too small to see.

prey An animal that is hunted by another.

tentacle A long feeler, used by an animal for sensing or to capture its food.

tide The rise and fall in sea level on the coast.

webbed feet When an animal has skin between its toes, so its feet work like paddles.

Further information

BOOKS

Look around you: Seaside
by Ruth Thomson, Wayland, 2007

First-Hand Science: Seashore
by Lynn Huggins-Cooper, Franklin Watts, 2003

WEBSITES

http://feeds.bbc.co.uk/wales/ wildaboutnature/explorer.shtml? Seaside
BBC Wales Nature site has clips and information about seashore life.

http://animal.discovery.com/guides /atoz/water.html
Animal Planet webpage on sea creatures has facts and clips about fish, seals, dolphins, sharks, octopus and more.

http://www.nationaltrust.org.uk/ main/w-chl/w countryside_ environment/w-coastline/ w-coastline-wildlife.htm
National Trust webpage on coastal wildlife has information on plants, birds, insects and the best places to spot wildlife by the sea.

Index